CHESTER'S EASIEST

G000080533

SIGHT-READING COURSE

By Carol Barratt

Illustrated by Sarah Lenton

Solve the sight-reading mystery

MASTER PLAN FOR PUPILS

Before you play each piece:
1. Read the clues, or hunt for them in the music
if none have been given.
2. Clap the piece, counting as you go.
3. **Imagine** yourself playing the piece, putting correct
fingers on correct notes as you count.

When you play each piece:
1. Make sure you keep your eyes on the **music**,
so that you don't miss any vital clues!
2. Try to look ahead. Do not look back.
3. Keep going, even if you make a mistake.
4. Enjoy yourselves!

TEACHER'S NOTE

Read through the notepads
with the pupil, and examine the clues
where they are given.

Encourage the pupil to learn by **feel**,
and not to look at the keyboard when
they are playing. Remember to stress
the importance of doing a little
sight-reading every day.

Order No.CH61219

Chester Music

(A division of Music Sales Limited)
8/9 Frith Street,London W1V 5TZ

STEPS

A **STEP** is when a note steps up or down a note.
(From line to next space, or space to next line.)

Up a Step = to the **right** on the keyboard.

→

Down a Step = to the **left** on the keyboard.

←

These Steps are also called Seconds.

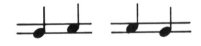

PLAY SOME 𝄞 STEPS

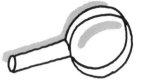 **STEPS UP**

 **STEPS DOWN**

Fingering ① ②

1.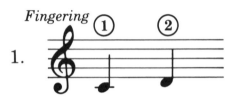

② ③

2.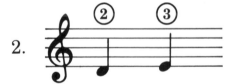

③ ④

3.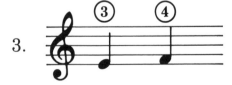

② ①

4.

③ ②

5.

④ ③

6.

WATCH YOUR STEPS!

Remember. Clap before you play. Imagine each piece through before you play.

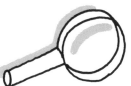

CLUES

1. How many Counts are there in the Time Signature?

2. After Count 2 in each Bar do you step up or down?

7.

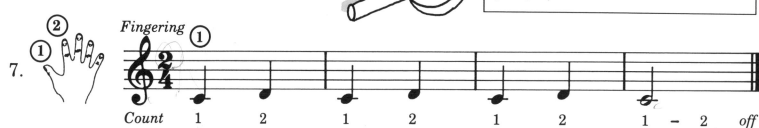

CLUES

1. How many Counts are there in the Time Signature?

2. How many Counts in a 𝅗𝅥 ?

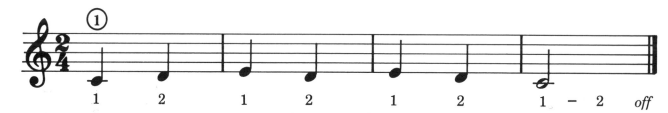

CLUES

1. Which finger does it start on?

2. How many Minims are there?

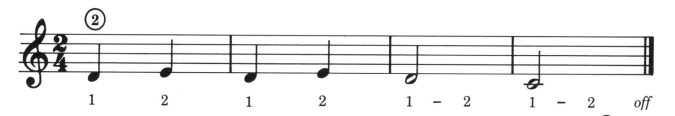

3

PLAY SOME 𝄢 STEPS

STEPS UP

STEPS 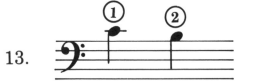 DOWN

Fingering ② ①

10.

13.

11.

14.

12.

15.

4

STEPPING FORWARD

16.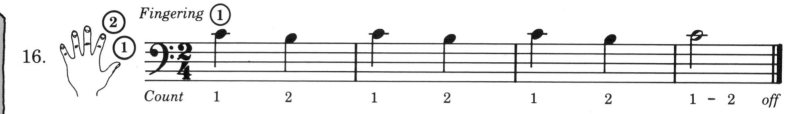

17.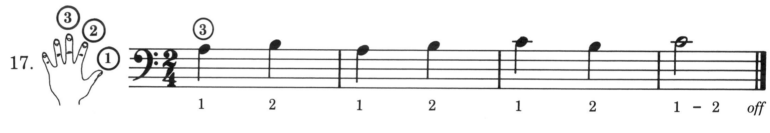

18.

ON THE TRAIL!

Watch the Clef. It could change.

Can you spot the repeated notes in Piece No. 22?

19.

Count   1   –   2   1   –   2   1   2   1   2   1   –   2

20.

1   –   2   3   –   4   1   –   2   3   –   4   1   –   2   3   –   4   1   –   2   –   3   –   4

21.

1   –   2   1   –   2   1   2   1   2   1   –   2

22.

1   –   2   3   –   4   1   –   2   3   –   4   1   –   2   3   –   4   1   –   2   –   3   –   4

LOOK OUT, LOOK OUT – FIFTH FINGER'S ABOUT!

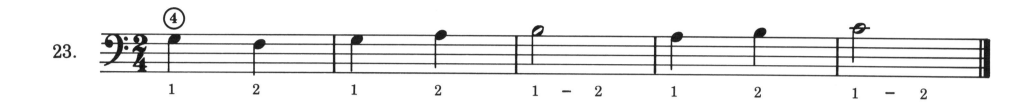

DOUBLE TROUBLE!

SKIPS

A **SKIP** is when a note skips to the next-but-one note up or down.
(From line to line, or space to space.)

Up a Skip = skip out **1** white key.

→

Down a Skip = skip out **1** white key.

←

These Skips are also called Thirds.

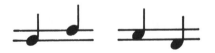

PLAY SOME 𝄞 SKIPS

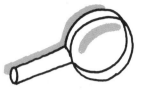 **UP**

SKIPS

SKIPS  **DOWN**

1.

2. (the staff with notes ② ④)

3. (the staff with notes ③ ⑤)

4.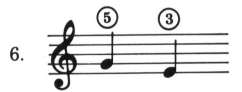

5. (the staff with notes ④ ②)

6. (the staff with notes ⑤ ③)

8

DON'T SKIP THE CLUES!

CLUES

1. How many Counts are there in the Time Signature?

2. After Count 2 in each Bar do you skip up or down?

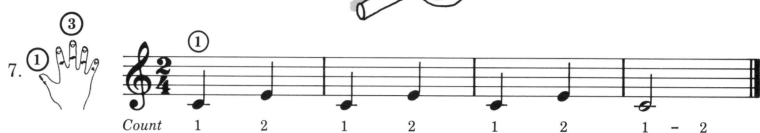

CLUES

1. How many Counts are there in the Time Signature?

2. Which fingers *won't* you be using?

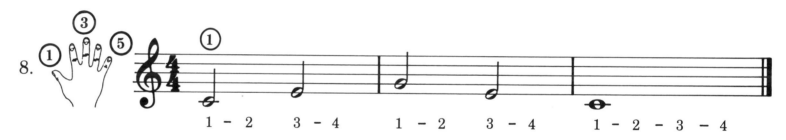

CLUES

1. How many Counts are there in the Time Signature?

2. What is the name of the repeated note?

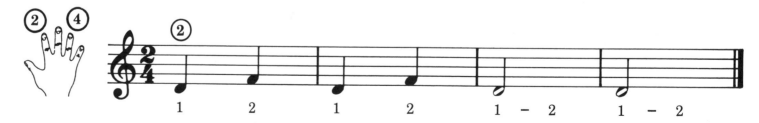

9

PLAY SOME 𝄢 SKIPS

 **UP**

SKIPS

SKIPS

DOWN

10.

13.

11.

14.

12.

15.

SKIP ALONG!

CLUES

1. How many Counts in each Bar?

2. After Count 2 in each Bar do you skip up or down?

16.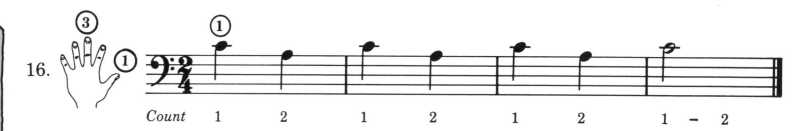

Count   1   2   1   2   1   2   1 - 2

CLUES

1. How many Counts are there in this new Time Signature?

2. How many Counts in a ♩.?

17.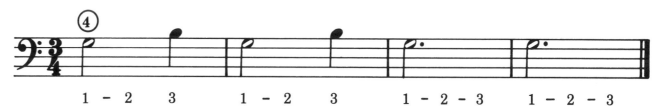

1 - 2   3   1 - 2   3   1 - 2 - 3   1 - 2 - 3

CLUES

1. How many Counts in each Bar?

2. Which fingers *won't* you be using?

18.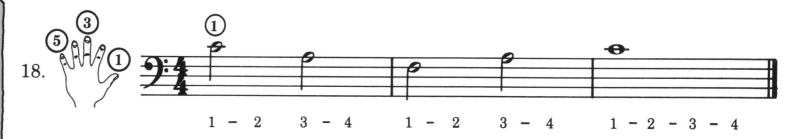

1 - 2   3 - 4   1 - 2   3 - 4   1 - 2 - 3 - 4

11

SKIP TO IT!

Keep an eye out for a few Steps among the Skips.

DOUBLE-TALK!

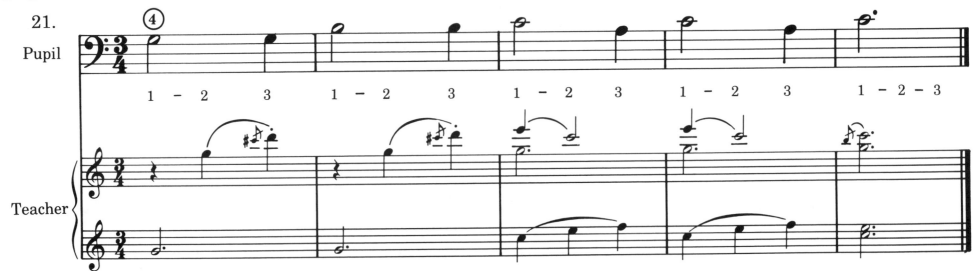

JUMPS

A **JUMP** is when a note jumps further than a skip.
At the moment, Jumps to look out for are Fourths and Fifths.

4ths → jump over **2** white keys.

4th

5ths → jump over **3** white keys.

5th

PLAY SOME 𝄞 JUMPS

 **UP**

JUMPS

JUMPS

DOWN

1. ① ④ 4th

2. ② ⑤ 4th

3. ① ⑤ 5th

4. ⑤ ② 4th

5. ④ ① 4th

6. ⑤ ① 5th

13

JUMP TO THE POINT!

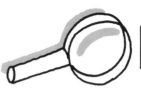

CLUES

1. How many Counts in each Bar?

2. What kind of Jumps are used – 4ths or 5ths?

CLUES

1. How many Counts in each Bar?

2. How many white keys do you jump over for a 5th?

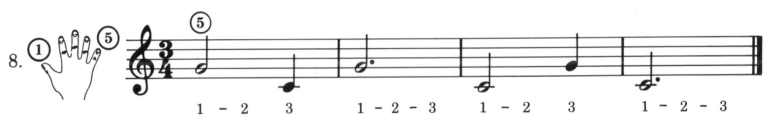

CLUES

1. How many Counts in each Bar?

2. What is the highest note?

14

PLAY SOME 𝄢 JUMPS

 **JUMPS** **UP**

 **JUMPS** **DOWN**

10.

11.

12.

13.

14.

15.

JUMP AT THE CHANCE

16.

17.

18.

16

EXAMINING THE EVIDENCE!

All music moves in Steps, Skips Jumps. Look out for them before y play.

Watch for new signs

The counts won't always be written in!

Circle all the Skips on this page and name all the notes.

BACK TRACK

Play these Steps, Skips and Jumps.

Watch the Clef.
It could change.

Fingering

1.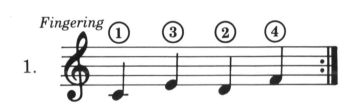

2.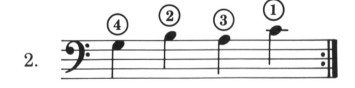

3.

4.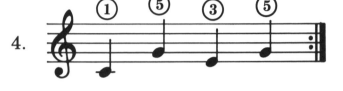

5.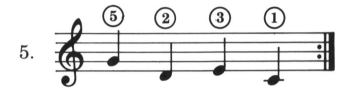

6.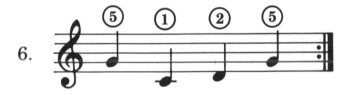

7.

8.

IN THE KNOW!

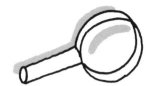

Remember. Clap before you play. Imagine each piece through before you play.

19

CLUES

1. Which Clef?

2. How many Counts are there in the Time Signature?

3. How many Skips are there?

9.

Fingering ①

Count   1   2   3   1 - 2   3   1   2   3   1 - 2 - 3

CLUES

1. Which Clef?

2. Chester doesn't always write in the Counts — How many Counts in a 𝅝?

3. What do *p* and *f* mean?

10.

CLUES

1. Which Clef?

2. What is the Interval in Bar 1 — a 4th or a 5th?

3. Which two Bars are the same?

11.

RESTS

A **REST** is a sign of silence. From now on they will be included in the pieces.

Don't forget to Count through the Rests — if Counts are given, the Rest Counts will be in brackets.

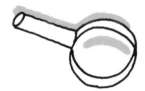

Look out for Rests in each piece before you play. Don't be caught out!

Don't hang on to a note when you should be resting!

TAKE A BREATHER!

Count out loud as you play.

1.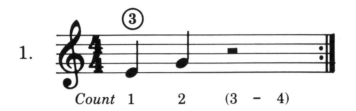

Count   1   2   (3 - 4)

2.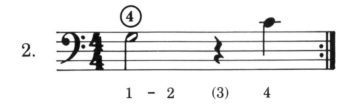

1 - 2   (3)   4

3.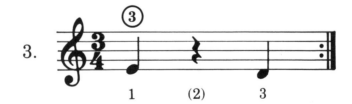

1   (2)   3

4.

(1 - 2 - 3) 1 2 3

5.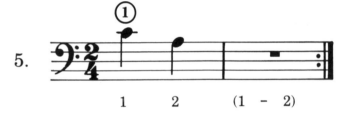

1   2   (1 - 2)

6.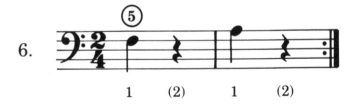

1 (2) 1 (2)

HANDS OFF!

Don't hang on when there should be **SILENCE.**

7.

8.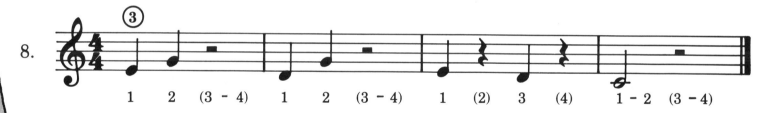

9.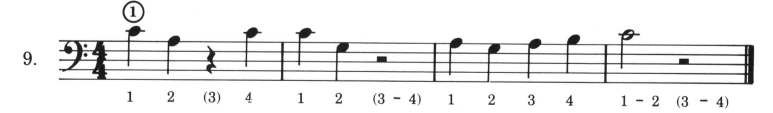

21

ARE YOU RESTING?

10.

11.
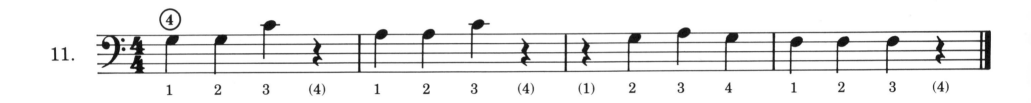

DOUBLED UP!

12.
Pupil

Teacher

B FLAT

B FLAT is the black key just below **B**.

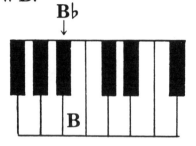

Until page 52, **B** flat will be in the left hand only.

As you spot a **B** Flat coming, move your hand **towards** the black key.

Be prepared!

FLATTEN DOWN!

Move **towards** the Flats.

1.

2.

3.

4.
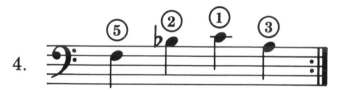

BLACK AND WHITE

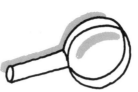

Don't forget – each ♭ sign lasts a Bar.

CLUES

1. How many B♭s are there?

2. What is the lowest note?

3. What kind of Rest is used?

5.

CLUES

1. How many Counts in each Bar?

2. Which two Bars have the same *rhythm*?

3. How many Skips are there?

6.

CLUES

1. What note does it start on?

2. How many B♭s are there?

3. How many Skips are there?

7.

24

F SHARP

F SHARP is the black key just above **F**.

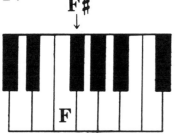

Until page 46, **F** sharp will be in the right hand only.

As you spot an **F** Sharp coming, move your hand **towards** the black key.

Be prepared!

SHARPEN UP!

Move **towards** the Sharps.

1.

2.

3.

4.

Remember FLATS always go down

←

Remember SHARPS always go up

→

Turn to page 21 and add a ♭ to the note B in exercise 9, and then play it through.

Add ♯'s to the notes F in exercise 10 on page 22, and then play it through.

25

KEEP A SHARP LOOK-OUT!

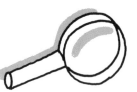

Don't forget – each ♯ sign lasts a Bar.

CLUES

1. How many **F♯**s are there?

2. What kind of Rest is used?

3. What is the Interval in Bar 3?

5.

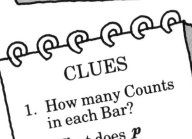

CLUES

1. How many Counts in each Bar?

2. What does *p* mean?

3. What kind of Rest is used?

6.

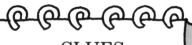

CLUES

1. Which two Bars are the same?

2. How many **F♯**s are there?

3. Can you spot the repeated note?

7.

CHESTER THE SNOOP

Your Code = **F** for Flat, **S** for Sharp. Track them down!

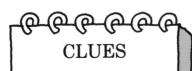

CLUES

1. Which Clef?
2. Is the Code **F** or **S**?
3. What does ◁ mean?

8.

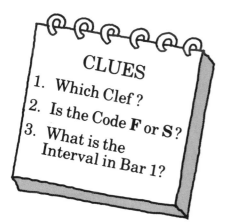

CLUES

1. Which Clef?
2. Is the Code **F** or **S**?
3. What is the Interval in Bar 1?

9.

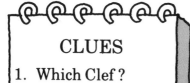

CLUES

1. Which Clef?
2. Is the Code **F** or **S**?
3. What kind of Rest is used?

10.

27

PHRASES

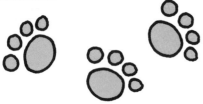

A **PHRASE-MARK** is a long curved line over a musical sentence.

From now on pieces may include Phrase-Marks. Imagine a breath at the end of each one, and lift your hand off briefly **without changing speed**.

To help you, the clue **//** has been added at first, so that you know where the Phrase finishes.

LIFT OFF! – SHORT PHRASES

Count out loud as you play, and keep a look-out for Repeat signs.

1.

2.
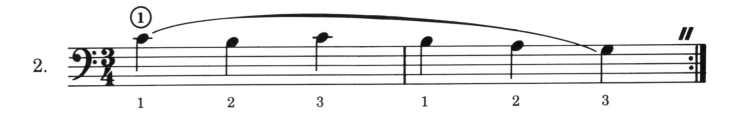

3.
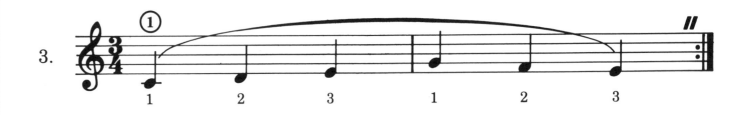

4.
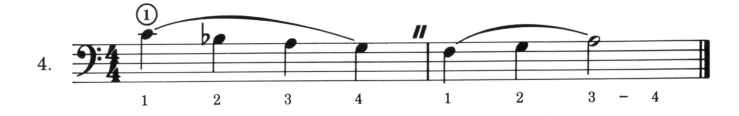

SENTENCED!

Before you play, say the words in strict time. Take a short breath after each sentence.

As you play, don't forget to lift your hand off briefly at the end of each Phrase-Mark.

CLUES

1. Which Clef ?

2. How many Bars in the first sentence?

3. Which finger do you use on the word 'Who'?

CLUES

1. Which Clef ?

2. Which Count does the second Phrase start on?

3. Which Rest is used?

5. Where were you last Sun - day? Who was with you?

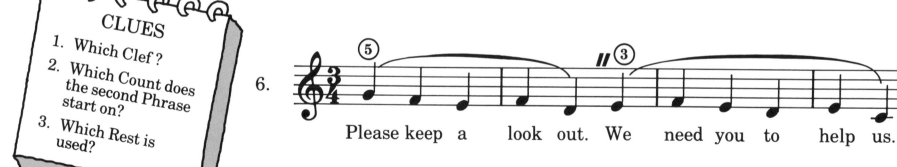

6. Please keep a look out. We need you to help us.

Have you answered the questions in Piece Number 5?

LOOK, BOTH WAYS
LOOK, BOTH HANDS

Don't hang on to the last note of the Phrase.

Quick tip. Tap out the rhythm using the right knee for the and the left knee for the

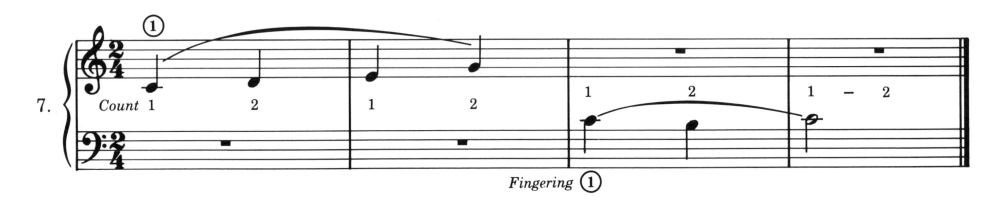

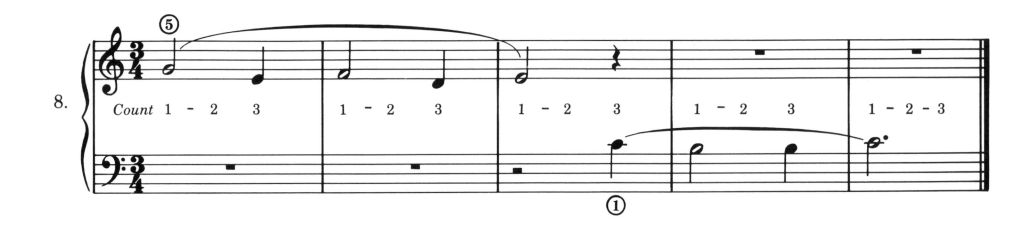

30

QUAVERS

A **QUAVER** is half the length of a Crotchet.

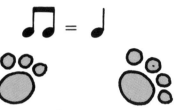

From now on pieces may include Quavers.

Count the Quavers like this:

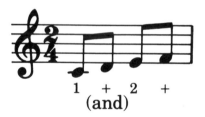

and follow the shape of the music as it goes up and down in Steps, Skips and Jumps.

Count out loud as you play Numbers 1–4.

QUAVERING!

1.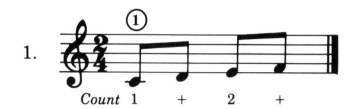
Count 1   +   2   +

3.
1   +   2   +

2.
1 + 2   1 + 2

4.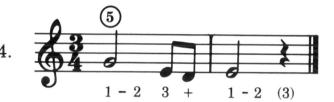
1 – 2   3   +   1 – 2   (3)

ON YOUR KNEES

5. Can you tap these rhythms on your knees?
Practise knees separately at first, and then try knees together!

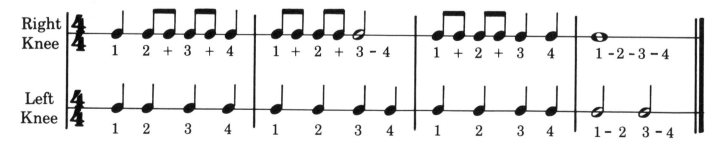

31

FRESH EVIDENCE

Remember. Clap it through.
Imagine it through.

CLUES

1. Which Clef?

2. How many Counts in a Bar?

3. How many Jumps can you see?

6.

1 + 2 + 3 + 4 + 1 + 2 + 3 - 4

CLUES

1. Which Clef?

2. Can you spot the repeated notes?

3. Which two Bars have the same *rhythm*?

7.

1 + 2 3 1 + 2 3 1 - 2 3 1 - 2 3

CLUES

1. Which Clef?

2. Which two Bars are the same?

3. Which Bars have the same *rhythm*?

8.

1 2 + 1 2 + 1 2 + 1 - 2

32

A COUNT OUT

Don't be caught out, there are Quavers about!

DOUBLE-QUICK!

Do you notice anything about Bars 1 and 3?

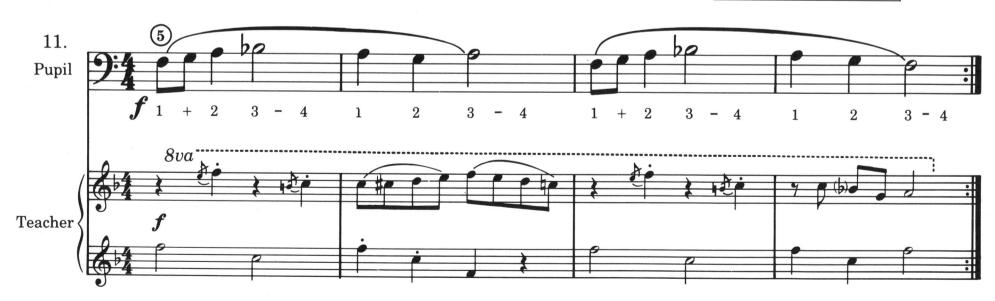

BETWEEN THE LINES

SEEING DOUBLE!

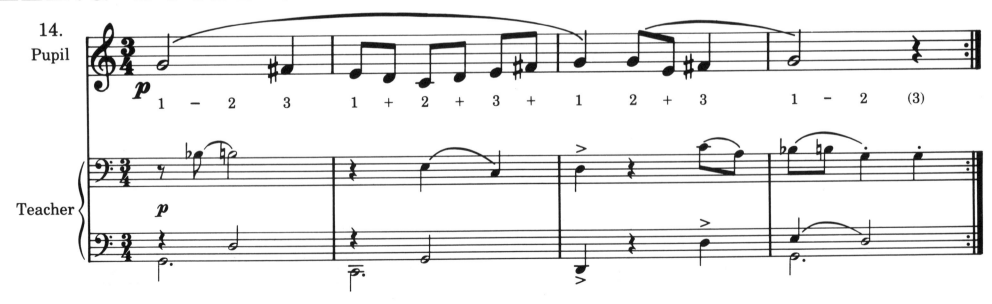

TIED NOTES

A TIE is a small curved line joining two of the same notes.

From now on pieces may include tied notes.

Play the first note, and then hold on and count the second note.

Please get wise –
Spot the ties!

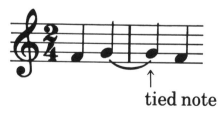

↑
tied note

Imagine that in the four exercises below, someone has stolen the ties. Play them at first as if there are **no** ties. Then play them as they should be – **with** the ties. Count out loud as you play.

1.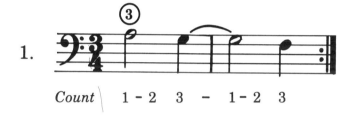

Count   1 - 2   3 - 1 - 2   3

2.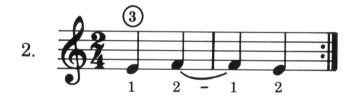

1   2 - 1   2

3.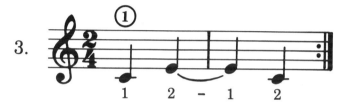

1   2 - 1   2

4.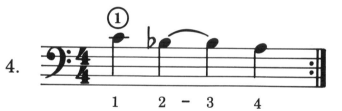

1   2 - 3   4

Turn back to page 32 – can you spot an exercise where you can draw in some ties?

35

A NEW LINE!

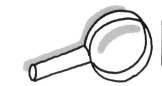

Remember. Clap it through.
Imagine it through.

CLUES

1. What is the letter-name of the tied note?
2. Which Rest is used?
3. What is the Interval marked with a Bracket? ⌐

5.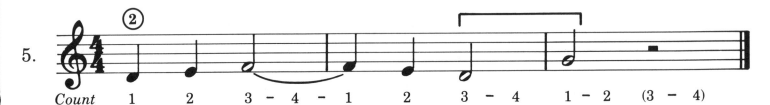

Count   1   2   3 - 4 - 1   2   3 - 4   1 - 2   (3 - 4)

CLUES

1. How many Counts in each Bar?
2. What are the letter-names of the tied notes?
3. Can you spot the repeated note?

6.

1   2   3 -   1   2   3   1 - 2 - 3 - 1 - 2 - 3

CLUES

1. Which two Bars have a *played* (not tied) note on the first Count?
2. Can you spot the repeated note?
3. Which Rest is used?

7.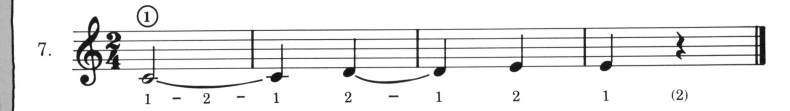

1 - 2 - 1   2 - 1   2   1   (2)

TIED UP!

Don't forget to do the 'Quick Tip' given on page 30.

8.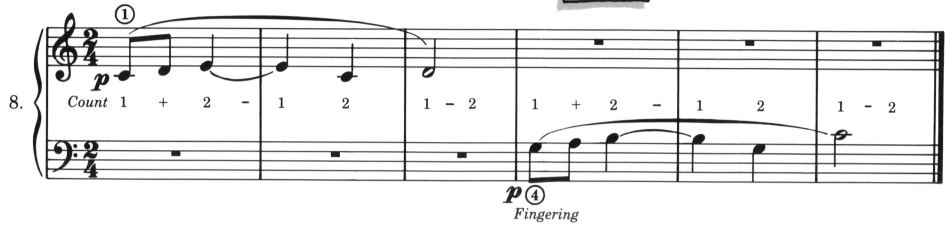

9.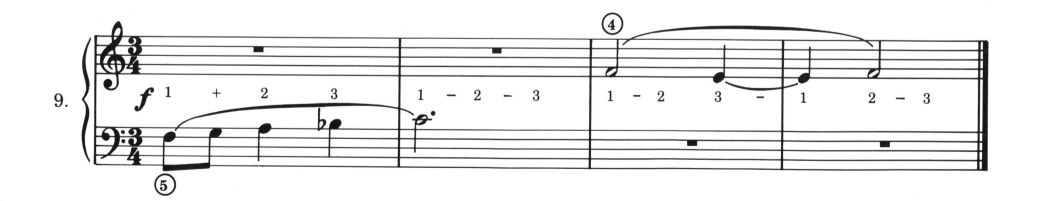

BREAKTHROUGH

Don't stop even if you stumble – Keep going.

DOUBLE AGENT!

BACK TRACK

WANTED

Count out loud as you play.
Lucky you – some of the
Counts are given!

REMINDER BOX

We've examined the following
in detail:

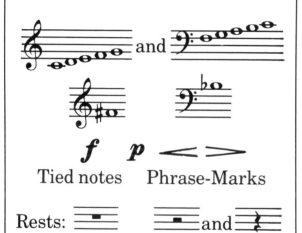

and

f **p** < >

Tied notes   Phrase-Marks

Rests:

and

Good sight-readers spot all the
evidence **before** they start to
play.

Follow the shape of the music as
it goes up and down in Steps,
Skips and Jumps.

Add two phrase marks to the first exercise.

1.

Fingering

Count **f** 1   +   2   1   +   2   1   2   +   1 - 2

2.

p 1 - 2   (3)   (1)   2   3   1 - 2   3   1 - 2   (3)

3.

f   **p**

KEY SIGNATURES

A **KEY SIGNATURE** is written after the Clef to show which ♯s or ♭s are needed in the piece.

All the **B**s in the piece will be **B♭**s.

All the **F**s in the piece will be **F♯**s.

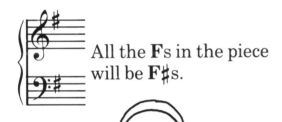

Look out for a Key Signature before you play. Then check out the notes which are changed by this Key Signature.

Be prepared!

LOOK BEFORE YOU LEAP!

Remember. Clap before you play. Imagine each piece through before you play.

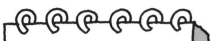

CLUES

1. What does the Key Signature tell you?

2. How many Counts in each Bar?

3. What is the Interval marked with ⌐‾⌐ ?

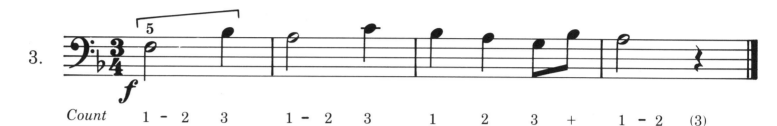

3.

Count   1 - 2   3   1 - 2   3   1   2   3   +   1 - 2   (3)

CLUES

1. What does the Key Signature tell you?

2. Where does the first Phrase-Mark end?

3. What should you do with your hand at the end of each Phrase-Mark?

4.

CLUES

1. What does the Key Signature tell you?

2. Do you *play* any ♯ or ♭ notes in this piece?

3. What happens at the very end of Bar 4?

5.

SIGNATURE TUNES!

SEEING DOUBLE?

Do you notice anything about Bars 1 and 3?

WANTED

42

FIRST AND LAST BARS

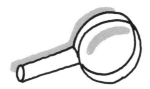

Remember. Start *counting* with Count 1 even if you don't actually start *playing* until later.

Pieces don't always start with Count 1.
The missing beats will be found in the last bar.
Always count yourself in, even if there is no beat to actually **play**.

1.

Count (1 2) 3   1   2   3   1 - 2

MUSIC DICTIONARY

You will often find an Italian word at the beginning of a piece of music to tell you how to play it. If you don't know what the word means, crack the code by looking for **Solutions** on the last page.

2.

(1) 2   1 + 2 +   1   2   1

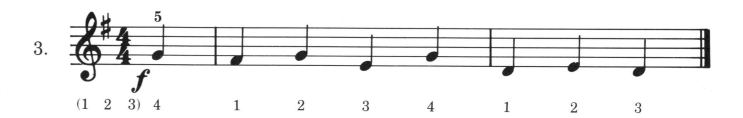

3.

(1 2 3) 4   1 2 3 4   1 2 3

Andante

4.

(1) 2 - 3   1 2 3   1 + 2 3   1

MAKING ENDS MEET!

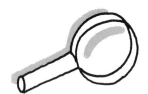

Don't hang on to the last note of the Phrase. Watch out for Repeat Signs.

Don't forget to do the 'Quick Tip' given on page 30.

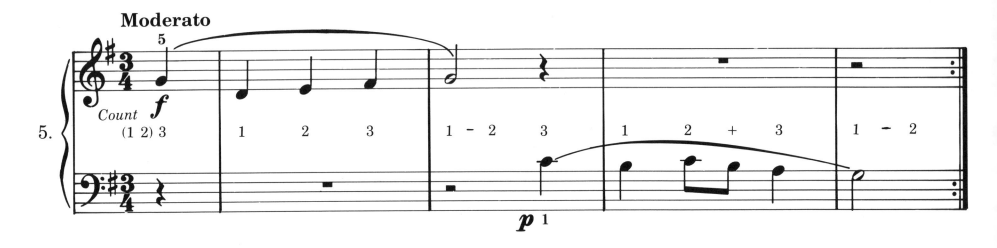

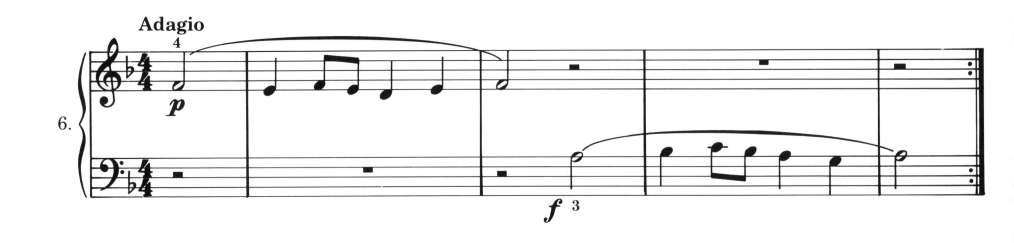

OCTAVES

An **OCTAVE** is the distance from one note to the next note with the same letter-name.

This Interval is eight notes.

NEW POSITION

New position: Left Hand plays **C–G**.

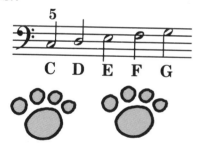

C   D   E   F   G

Hunt for the **C** an Octave below **Middle C** and put your fifth finger on it.

This gives you three new notes.

A CHANGE OF PLAN

Andante

1.

Moderato

2.

How smart are you? Try playing Piece No.2 an Octave lower than it is written.

45

TAKING THE PLUNGE!

Do you know this tune?

CLUES
1. Which Rest is used?
2. What does Allegro mean?
3. What does *legato* mean?

Allegro

3.

CLUES
1. On which Count do you start to play?
2. What is the letter-name of the note on the first Count 1?
3. What happens at * '

Andante

4.

CLUES
1. Which Rest is used?
2. How many **E♭**s are there?
3. What is the Interval marked with ⌐ ?

Moderato

5.

ACCIDENTALS

♮ is a **NATURAL SIGN.** This cancels a ♯ or a ♭ sign.

Any sign (♯, ♭ or ♮) that is not in the Key Signature is called an **ACCIDENTAL.**

Look for Accidentals before you **play.**

Then work out which finger plays which Accidental. Always move in **towards** the black keys.

Be prepared!

Adagio

1.

Andante

2.

Moderato

3.

Count (1 2) 3   4   1   2   3   4   1 - 2   3 - 4 - 1 - 2

Mysteriously

4.

47

COMPLETELY ACCIDENTAL!

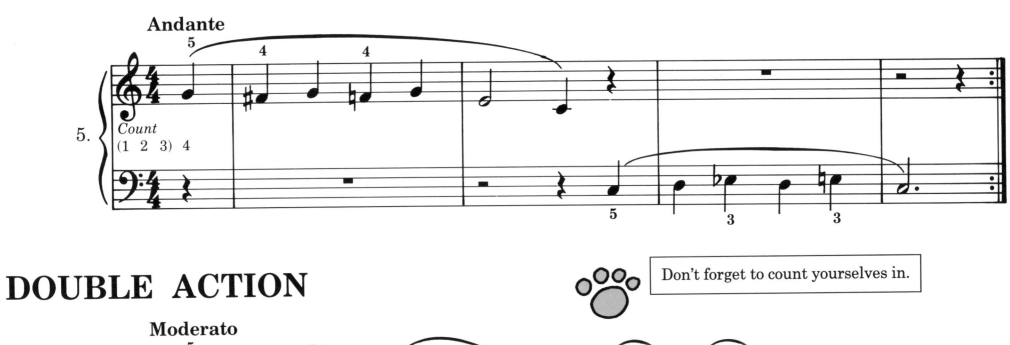

DOUBLE ACTION

Don't forget to count yourselves in.

NEW POSITION

New Position: Right Hand plays **G – D**.

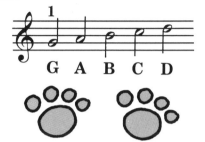

G A B C D

Put your first finger on **G** instead of your fifth finger. This gives you four new notes.

NEW SIGNS

⌒ = **PAUSE**

When you have played the note with ⌒ above it, say "Pause" in your head before playing the next note.

If you don't know how to play these notes, look at the last page.

Allegro

1.

Andante

2.

Moderato

3.

Count 1 2 3 1 2 - 3 Pause 1 2 3 1 - 2 (3)

Allegro

4.

49

UP AND AWAY IN TIME TO PLAY

CLUES

1. What does the Key Signature tell you?
2. Which Rest is used?
3. What does Andante mean?

5.

CLUES

1. On which Count do you start to play?
2. How many Staccato notes are there?
3. What does > mean?

6.

CLUES

1. How many tied notes can you spot?
2. What happens on the last note?
3. What does Moderato mean?

7.

QUAVER RESTS

𝄾 = **QUAVER REST**

Ask the pupil to sing the rhythms of Pieces **1–3** on **one note** so that he/she can 'hear' where the silences should come. Count aloud as they are being sung.

Remember – Don't hang on to a note when you should be resting!

Sadly

1.

Count   *p*   1   2   (+)   1   2   (+)   (1)   +   2   +   1   (+)   2   (+)

Andante

2.

f   1   2   (+   3   1)   2   3   1   2   (+   3)

Allegro

3.

p   1   +   2   (+)   1   +   2   (+)   (1)   +   2   +   1 - 2

SUMMING UP

Important. Expression marks will make the music sound much more interesting, so remember to use them.

COLLECT THE EVIDENCE

CLUES
1. What is the name of the Accidental in Bar 1?
2. What does ♩ mean?
3. What does Andante mean?

8.

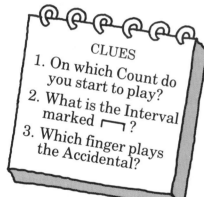

CLUES
1. On which Count do you start to play?
2. What is the Interval marked ⌐—⌐?
3. Which finger plays the Accidental?

9.

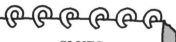

CLUES
1. How many tied notes can you spot?
2. What happens on the last two beats?
3. How many Staccato notes are there?

10.

TAKE NOTE!

Can you spot the Octave **G** between the hands in Piece No. 11?

DOUBLE HANDED

DON'T LOSE TRACK!

Look out! The  starts first.

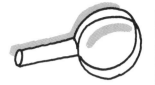

Remember. Keep counting and keep going even of you make a mistake.

DOUBLE CROSS

The teacher has to play on either side of the pupil's part. Try not to get tangled up!

MIDDLE B and MIDDLE D

In this position, **Middle Cs** will be played by Finger 2.

MIDDLE B can also be written in the Treble Clef – a Step below **Middle C.**

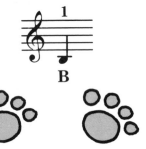

Middle D can also be written in the Bass Clef – a Step above **Middle C.**

At the moment they will be played with Finger 1.

Look out for these notes below and above the Staves.

Andante

1.

Allegro

2.

Adagio

3.

Moderato

4.

MIDDLE MEN

If you don't know what the
Time Signature **C** means,
look at the last page.

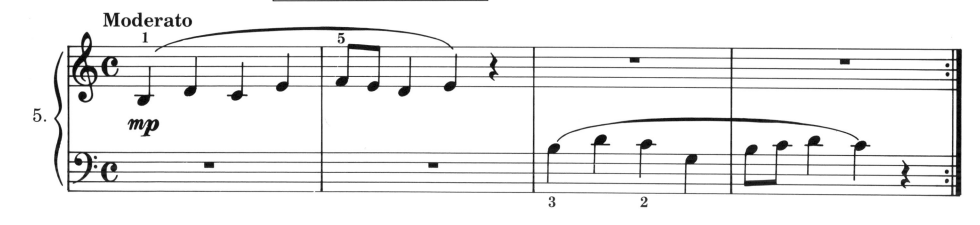

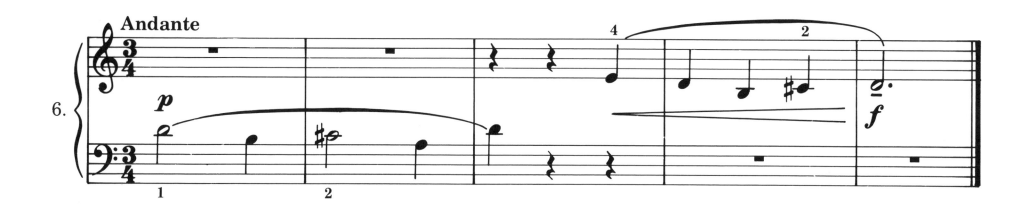

DOTTED CROTCHETS

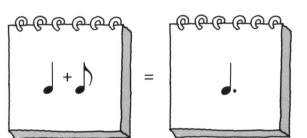

A **DOTTED CROTCHET:**

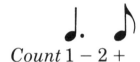

Hold on to the dot − it is half a Count. The other half of the Count could be ♪ or 𝄽

Count 1 − 2 +

Count 1 − 2 (+)

1. Clap the Pieces counting out loud.
2. Sing the rhythms on one note before you play.

Moderato

1.

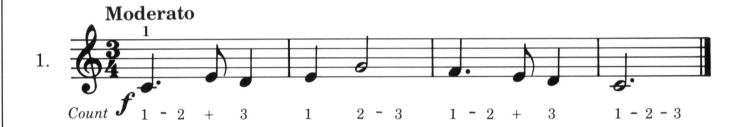

Count ***f*** 1 - 2 + 3   1   2 - 3   1 - 2 + 3   1 - 2 - 3

Andante

2.

p 1 - 2 + 3   4   1 - 2 + 3 - 4 (+)   1 - 2 + 3 - 4

Tap out the rhythms on page 59 on your knee:
(𝄞 = right knee, 𝄢 = left knee).

If you can, tap ♩ beats at the same time on your other knee. Wow!

58

SPOT THE DOTS

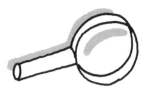

Watch the dots. Some are Staccato dots.

With a swing

3.

Count 1 - 2   +   3   1 - 2   +   3   1   2 - 3   +   1 - 2   (3)

Moderato

4.

Allegro

5.

Brightly

6.

59

FREE POSITIONS

Remember. Clap it through.
Imagine it through.

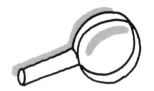

Set Hand Positions will not necessarily be used from now on.

Make sure that you know these notes:

B C D E F G A B C D E

C D E F G A B C D

Always look carefully at the first note of each phrase to work out where you should be playing.

You may need to stretch your hand or jump more than 5 notes from now on.

Brightly

1.

Andante

2.

Legato

3.

Allegro

4.

60

MOVING TARGETS!

CLUES

1. What does Adagio mean?
2. What is the letter-name of the top note?
3. What happens to Finger 2 on the Accidental?

5.

CLUES

1. What does Andante mean?
2. What do you do when you see the word Rit.?
3. What does *mf* mean?

6.

CLUES

1. What does *ff* mean?
2. What does > mean?
3. What is the Interval between the last two notes?

7.

61

AIM CAREFULLY

Remember. Clap it through.
Imagine it through.

INSIDE STORY

Look – both hands together!

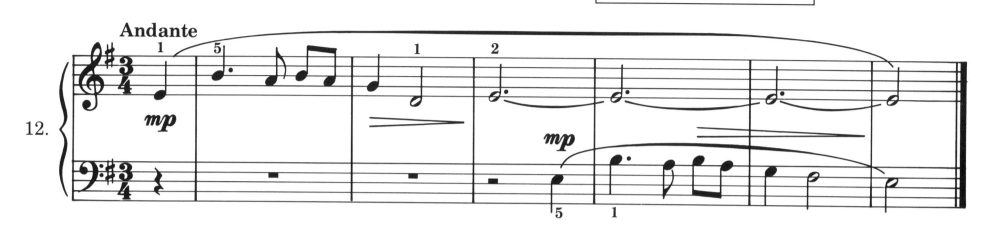

DOUBLE SHUFFLE
(A kind of Hornpipe)

Look at the Key Signature.
Can you spot anything new?

GET CRACKING!

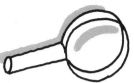

Move your eyes **along** the music and try to look a bar ahead. Don't miss a clue!

SOLUTIONS

Some WORDS and SIGNS used in this book

mp   (mezzo piano) → Moderately Soft

mf   (mezzo forte) → Moderately Loud

p   (piano) → Soft

f   (forte) → Loud

pp   (pianissimo) → Very Soft

ff   (fortissimo) → Very Loud

Adagio → Slow

Andante → Fairly Slow

Moderato → Moderate Speed

Allegro → Fast

→ Staccato (a dot above or below a note) To be played short and crisp

→ Tenuto – stress the note

→ Accent – play slightly louder than the other notes

C → Common Time **4/4**

Legato → Play Smoothly

64   Printed in the United Kingdom by Caligraving Limited, Thetford, Norfolk.

6/01 (40481)